Ephesus Travel Guide 2023-2024

A Comprehensive Guide to Exploring the Rich Heritage of the City

Bruce Terry

Bruce Terry

Copyright © 2023 Bruce Terry All rights reserved.

No part of this book may be reproduced, stored in a retrieval system, or transmitted in any form or by any means electronic, mechanical, photocopying, recording, scanning, or otherwise without the prior written permission of the publisher.

The work contained herein is the sole property of the author and may not be reproduced or copied in any form without express permission from the author. All information is provided as is, without any warranty of any kind, liability expressly disclaimed. The publisher and the author disclaim any liability for any loss, risk, or damage allegedly arising from the use, application, or interpretation of the content herein.

Bruce Terry

TABLE OF CONTENTS

INTRODUCTION 7

    10 REASONS WHY YOU SHOULD VISIT EPHESUS 8

CHAPTER 1 11

    GETTING TO EPHESUS.. 11

- Getting to Ephesus 11

CHAPTER 2 13

    BEST TIME TO VISIT EPHESUS 13

CHAPTER 3 15

    EXPLORING THE ANCIENT CITY OF EPHESUS 15

- THE LIBRARY OF CELSUS 15

    THE GREAT THEATER OF EPHESUS 18

- THE TEMPLE OF ARTEMIS 21

CHAPTER 4 25

    OTHER HISTORICAL SITES IN THE SURROUNDING AREA 25

- THE HOUSE OF THE VIRGIN MARY 25
- THE BASILICA OF ST. JOHN 28
- THE EPHESUS ARCHAEOLOGICAL MUSEUMS 31

CHAPTER 5 35

ACCOMMODATION OPTIONS IN EPHESUS 35

- LUXURY HOTELS AND RESORTS 35
- COZY BED AND BREAKFAST 40
- BOUTIQUE HOTELS WITH LOCAL CHARM 43

CHAPTER 6 47

LOCAL CUISINES AND DINING 47

- TRADITIONAL TURKISH DISHES 47
- MUST-TRY RESTAURANTS IN EPHESUS 49

CHAPTER 7 53

OUTDOOR ACTIVITIES AND EXCURSIONS 53

- HIKING AND NATURE WALKS 53
- BOAT TOURS ALONG THE AEGEAN COAST 57
- EXPLORING THE ANCIENT CITY OF PRIENE 60

CHAPTER 8 65

SHOPPING IN EPHESUS 65

- LOCAL HANDICRAFTS AND SOUVENIRS 65
- EPHESUS' STREET MARKETS 68
- SHOPPING CENTERS AND MALLS 70

CHAPTER 9 73

EPHESUS' NIGHTLIFE AND ENTERTAINMENT 73

- BARS AND CLUBS 73
- TRADITIONAL TURKISH MUSIC AND DANCE SHOW 76

EVENING STROLLS AND PROMENADES 79

CHAPTER 10 81

PRACTICAL TIPS FOR TRAVELING TO EPHESUS 81

- VISA AND ENTRY REQUIREMENTS 81
- HEALTH AND SAFETY PRECAUTIONS 83
- TRANSPORTATION OPTIONS WITHIN EPHESUS 86

CONCLUSION 89

Bruce Terry

EPHESUS TRAVEL GUIDE 2023-2024

Bruce Terry

INTRODUCTION

Welcome to Ephesus, the captivating ancient city where history breathes and the heritage of civilizations past comes to life. As we continue on this incredible voyage through time, I urge you to enter a place where the old world meets the present, and where echoes of grandeur past may be found in every stone and pillar. As your Ephesus guide in 2023-2024, I vow to reveal the mysteries of this awe-inspiring archaeological marvel, presenting you with an extraordinary experience that will transport you back in time to a place where gods and humans once walked hand in hand.

Ephesus, located in modern-day Turkey, is a tribute to the inventiveness and intelligence of the people who once inhabited this extraordinary city. Every nook of Ephesus is embellished with stories of empires, wars, and cultural interchange, from the grandeur of the Library of Celsus to the beauty of the Great Theatre. This archaeological treasure, which dates back to the 10th century BC, has millennia of history inside its ancient walls.

But this isn't simply a trip down memory lane. Ephesus hums with activity, providing a dynamic environment in which tradition and modernity coexist together. Explore the busy marketplaces, sample the delectable flavors of Turkish food, and connect with the friendly inhabitants who proudly carry the flame of their ancestors' history.

Bruce Terry

As your own Ephesus tour guide, I will reveal the lesser-known treasures, secret passages, and unexplored nooks of this ancient city, ensuring that you see a side of Ephesus that few have seen before. Ephesus has something remarkable to offer everyone, whether you're a history buff, an inquisitive traveler, or a person seeking spiritual connection.

So strap in for a journey back in time, where the stories of Ephesus will capture your mind and leave an unforgettable stamp on your heart. Join me as we travel across time and space, immersing ourselves in the unique allure of Ephesus in the years 2023-2024. Let us go on this memorable journey together, and see the glories of Ephesus unfold before our eyes.

10 REASONS WHY YOU SHOULD VISIT EPHESUS

Ancient Remains & Archaeological Sites: Ephesus has an assortment of well-preserved ancient remains, including the famous Library of Celsus, the Great Theatre, the Temple of Artemis (one of the Seven Wonders of the Ancient World), and the Terrace Houses. Exploring these old monuments provides a unique view into the grandeur and elegance of the former civilizations.

Library of Celsus: The Library of Celsus serves as a symbolic reflection of the city's academic and cultural significance. This renowned monument is a wonder of Roman construction, featuring beautiful carvings and sculptures, making it a favored destination for history aficionados and photographers.

The Great Theatre: As one of the greatest Roman theaters ever erected, the Great Theatre in Ephesus could seat up to 25,000 people. Today, the theater is still utilized for concerts and events, enabling visitors to enjoy the wonderful acoustics of the old amphitheater.

Temple of Artemis: Visiting the remnants of the Temple of Artemis, devoted to the ancient Greek goddess of the hunt, lends a dimension of mysticism and spirituality to the excursion. While just a few columns remain intact, the site possesses tremendous historical and theological value.

Terrace Houses (Ephesus Houses): For a more personal peek into the everyday life of the ancient wealthy, the Terrace Houses give a compelling perspective. These well-preserved residential structures include magnificent paintings, elaborate mosaics, and innovative architectural elements.

Ancient City design: Ephesus is recognized for its well-structured urban design, with paved streets, a sophisticated sewage system, and an efficient water supply system. Studying this ancient city's layout gives great insights into urbanization and engineering methods of antiquity.

Bruce Terry

Historical Significance: As one of the twelve towns of the Ionian League, Ephesus played a vital role in creating the cultural and political environment of ancient Anatolia. The city experienced the presence of renowned personalities such as Alexander the Great, Saint Paul, and the Virgin Mary, contributing to its historical attraction.

Religious Significance: Ephesus is strongly identified with early Christianity, and it is believed that the Virgin Mary spent her final years in a modest stone cottage on Mount Koressos, today a renowned pilgrimage destination known as the cottage of the Virgin Mary. The city was also referenced in the Bible's Book of Revelation.

Ephesian Artemis and the Ephesus Museum: The Ephesus Archaeological Museum displays a significant collection of items excavated from the ancient city, including the famed statue of Artemis of Ephesus. This provides visitors the chance to learn about the religious rituals and creative accomplishments of the past.

Nearby Attractions: Ephesus's strategic position offers it a great base to visit other spectacular sites in Turkey, such as the magnificent beaches of Kusadasi, the ancient city of Hierapolis, the natural wonder of Pamukkale, and the scenic village of Selcuk.

Bruce Terry

CHAPTER 1

GETTING TO EPHESUS

- **Getting to Ephesus**

a. **By Air**

The most usual method to reach Ephesus is via flying into one of the surrounding airports. Two main airports should be taken into account:

Izmir Adnan Menderes Airport (ADB): This is the nearest major airport to Ephesus, situated roughly 68 kilometers (42 miles) away. It is well-connected to key international and local locations, making it the favored option for most passengers. From the airport, you may reach Ephesus via several transportation choices, including buses, shuttles, and taxis.

Bodrum Milas Airport (BJV): While less accessible than Izmir Airport, Bodrum Airport is another choice, especially if you intend to tour the Aegean coast and other regions of Turkey before or after visiting Ephesus. The distance from Bodrum Airport to Ephesus is roughly 225 kilometers (140 miles), and transportation choices include buses and rental automobiles.

Bruce Terry

b. By Train

Ephesus does not have a railway station within the near neighborhood. However, if you prefer rail travel, you may take a train to Selçuk, the town closest to Ephesus. Selçuk is just a few kilometers away from the ancient site, and daily trains link it to important towns like Izmir and Denizli. From the Selçuk railway station, you may take a short taxi or bus trip to reach Ephesus.

c. By Bus

A large network of buses links Ephesus to several towns in Turkey. The region's major bus station is in Selçuk, making it easy for passengers to come by bus. There are frequent bus routes from Izmir, Istanbul, Bodrum, and other important Turkish cities. The buses are typically pleasant, and the ride may be a terrific chance to experience the gorgeous Turkish countryside.

d. By Car

If you prefer the freedom of driving, you may hire a vehicle from major towns or airports in Turkey. The travel to Ephesus from Izmir takes roughly an hour along the E87 motorway. The roads are typically well-maintained, and there are visible signs to take you to the archaeological site.

Bruce Terry

CHAPTER 2

BEST TIME TO VISIT EPHESUS

1. *Weather and Climate:* The weather and climate are key aspects to consider while arranging a vacation to Ephesus. The area has a Mediterranean climate, typified by hot, dry summers and warm, rainy winters. The optimum season to visit Ephesus in terms of weather is during the spring (April to June) and fall (September to October). During these months, temperatures are normally nice, ranging from 15°C to 25°C (59°F to 77°F), making it acceptable for touring the historic ruins and outdoor areas.

2. *Crowds and Tourist Season:* Another element to consider is the tourist season and the crowds at Ephesus. The biggest tourist season is throughout the summer months (July to August). During this period, the place may grow quite busy, and temperatures can surge beyond 30°C (86°F).

If you want a more quiet and serene experience, it's better to skip the high season and plan your vacation in the shoulder months, such as April, May, September, and October. Visiting at these times enables you to see Ephesus without the overwhelming crowds, making it easier to appreciate the historical value of the area.

3. *Special Events and Festivals:* Ephesus offers many cultural events and festivals throughout the year. The Ephesus Festival, held yearly

Bruce Terry

in May and June, is a festival of classical music and performances that take place in the historic amphitheater, adding a new depth to your stay. Additionally, the International Izmir Festival, held in June and July, typically involves concerts, theatrical plays, and cultural activities in neighboring Izmir, which is readily accessible from Ephesus.

4. *Prices & Accommodation:* Traveling during the off-peak season may also be helpful in terms of price. Accommodation rates tend to be cheaper, and you may get better bargains on flights and travel packages. By skipping the busy season, you may save money and perhaps increase your stay to a more opulent alternative without breaking the bank.

5. *Blossoming Flora:* For nature aficionados and photographers, visiting Ephesus during the spring gives an added delight - the blossoming flora. The countryside surrounding Ephesus erupts with brilliant flowers and lush vegetation throughout this season, offering a stunning background to the ancient remains and enriching the whole experience.

6. *Daylight Hours:* Considering the daylight hours is vital, particularly if you intend to make the most of your vacation and tour Ephesus completely. The longest days with abundant sunshine come around late spring and early fall, providing you with more time to explore the ancient site and acquire magnificent images.

Bruce Terry

CHAPTER 3

EXPLORING THE ANCIENT CITY OF EPHESUS

• THE LIBRARY OF CELSUS

1. **History and Significance:**

A Brief History: The Library of Celsus was established in the 2nd century AD, during the Roman era, by Gaius Julius Aquila in honor of his father, Celsus Polemaeanus, a distinguished Roman senator and scholar. It functioned as both a tomb for Celsus and a library to store an extraordinary collection of scrolls and manuscripts.

Architectural Marvel: The library's design is a superb example of Roman architecture, defined by its majestic façade and two-storied construction. The exterior has stunning Corinthian-style columns, exquisite sculptures, and detailed reliefs, representing the grandeur of the old city.

2. **Location and Access:**

Ephesus Location: The Library of Celsus is located in Ephesus, an ancient Greek city on the western coast of present-day Turkey, near Selçuk.

Accessibility: Ephesus is readily accessible from major adjacent cities like Izmir and Kusadasi. Visitors may access the location via automobile, public transportation, or guided excursions.

3. Planning Your Visit:

Best Time to Visit: The optimum time to see Ephesus and the Library of Celsus is during the spring (April to June) and fall (September to November) when the weather is moderate, and tourist crowds are less dense.

Entry Tickets: You may buy tickets at the entry or online in advance to avoid lengthy lineups.

Guided Tours: Consider taking a guided tour to acquire vital insights into the history and importance of the Library of Celsus and other sites inside Ephesus.

4. Exploring the Library of Celsus:

Architectural Features: Marvel at the magnificently rebuilt front, studded with figures depicting wisdom (Sophia), understanding (Episteme), intellect (Ennoia), and morality (Arete). Observe the elaborate reliefs showing numerous mythical and historical situations.

The Celsus Mausoleum: Take a minute to observe the mausoleum of Celsus, which formerly contained his remains and remains a notable component of the library's construction.

Bruce Terry

Interior: While the original interior was destroyed, you may envision the grandeur of the past as you wander through the passageways that once contained innumerable rare scrolls and manuscripts.

6. Nearby Attractions:

The Grand Theater: After touring the Library of Celsus, travel to the neighboring Grand Theater, one of the biggest ancient theaters in Anatolia, with a capacity of nearly 24,000 people.

Temple of Artemis: Don't miss the opportunity to explore the remnants of the Temple of Artemis, one of the Seven Wonders of the Ancient World, situated a short distance away.

6. Practical Tips:

Wear Comfortable Shoes: The location requires a good bit of walking, so wear comfortable footwear.

Sun Protection: The location may become fairly hot, so bring sunscreen, a hat, and a drink to remain hydrated.

Respect the Site: The Library of Celsus is a rare historical asset; abstain from harming or destroying any items or buildings.

Bruce Terry

THE GREAT THEATER OF EPHESUS

1. History and Significance

The Great Theater of Ephesus, sometimes known simply as the Ephesus Theater, was established during the Hellenistic era, about the 3rd century BC, and subsequently enlarged and refurbished by the Romans in the 1st century AD. It was a vital element of the ancient city of Ephesus, which was one of the biggest and most significant towns in the Roman Empire.

The theater was utilized for different reasons, including theatrical performances, concerts, religious events, and political meetings. It could hold up to 25,000 people, making it one of the biggest theaters of its time. The Great Theater of Ephesus also retains historical importance as the location where the riot against the Apostle Paul happened, as recounted in the New Testament.

2. How to Get There

2.1. Location

The Great Theater of Ephesus is located in Selcuk, a town in the Izmir region of Turkey. It is around 3 kilometers (1.9 miles) from the heart of Selcuk and about 18 kilometers (11.2 miles) from the seaside city of Kusadasi.

2.2. *Transportation by Air*: The closest major airport is the Izmir Adnan Menderes Airport (ADB), which is well-connected to major cities in Turkey and international destinations. From Izmir, you may take a cab or hire a vehicle to reach Ephesus.

By rail/Bus: Selcuk is accessible by rail from Izmir, and the travel takes approximately an hour. Alternatively, you may take a bus from big cities like Izmir or Kusadasi to Selcuk.

By vehicle: If you prefer driving, you may hire a vehicle in Izmir or Kusadasi and follow the well-marked directions to Ephesus.

3. **What to Expect**

3.1. *Architecture*

The Great Theater of Ephesus is a spectacular example of Roman architecture. It is constructed into the slope of Mount Pion, affording a spectacular background of the surrounding area. The theater consists of three primary sections: the audience area (cavea), the stage (orchestra), and the backstage (scaenae frons). The majestic front of the stage structure, embellished with columns and sculptures, formerly exhibited the grandeur of ancient shows.

3.2. *Acoustics*

One of the most notable qualities of the theater is its superb acoustics. Even today, the construction enables a speaker's voice to be heard well by the whole audience without the need for contemporary amplification. Visitors typically stand in the middle of the stage to test this unusual sonic phenomenon.

3.3. *Spectacular Views*

Besides the historical importance and architectural wonder, the Great Theater of Ephesus provides tourists with stunning panoramic views of the ancient city and the surrounding countryside. Don't forget to grab your camera to record these wonderful moments.

4. Essential Tips for Visiting

4.1. *Wear Comfortable Clothing*

Exploring the remains of Ephesus may be physically hard, so bring comfortable shoes and lightweight clothes ideal for walking and climbing stairs.

4.2. *Visit Early or Late in the Day*

To avoid enormous crowds and the heat of the day, try visiting the Great Theater of Ephesus early in the morning or later in the afternoon.

4.3. *Engage a Tour Guide*

Hiring a skilled tour guide can increase your experience as they can give historical background and great tales about the location.

Bruce Terry

4.4. *Respect the Site*

While touring the theater, note that it is a protected archaeological site. Please avoid touching or climbing on the old buildings to preserve them for future generations.

• THE TEMPLE OF ARTEMIS

1. History and Significance

The Temple of Artemis was erected in the ancient city of Ephesus around the 6th century BCE. It was planned by the Greek architect Chersiphron and finished by his son Metagenes. The temple was huge, stretching roughly 377 feet (115 meters) long and 180 feet (55 meters) broad, having 127 columns, each towering at an astonishing height of 60 feet (18 meters).

Artemis, the Greek goddess of hunting, wildness, and fertility, was greatly venerated in ancient times, and her temple at Ephesus became one of the most famous religious centers in the Hellenistic world. Pilgrims and tradesmen from diverse places came to pay tribute to the goddess and seek her favors.

2. Location

The Temple of Artemis is located just outside the current town of Selcuk in Izmir Province, Turkey. The precise site is inside the bounds of Ephesus, a once-thriving ancient city that was a significant element of the Roman and Greek civilizations.

3. **Getting There**

a. *By Air*

If you are coming from an overseas location, the closest major airport is the Izmir Adnan Menderes Airport (ADB). From the airport, you may rent a cab or utilize public transit to reach Selcuk.

b. *By Train*

Selcuk is well-connected by rail from Izmir, giving it a handy alternative for those arriving from inside Turkey. The Selcuk railway station is adjacent to the town center, making it convenient to access the Temple of Artemis.

c. *By Road*

Selcuk is accessible by road, and there are frequent buses that link the town to major cities in Turkey. If you prefer driving, you may hire a vehicle and follow the well-marked road markers to reach the location.

4. **Entrance Fees and Opening Hours**

Before arranging your visit, it's vital to verify the current admission prices and opening hours of the Temple of Artemis. This

Bruce Terry

information may change dependent on the season and any current restoration work.

5. Exploring the Temple of Artemis

As you set foot upon the archaeological site of the Temple of Artemis, you'll be whisked back in time to ancient Greece. Though just a few columns remain standing now, it's still feasible to appreciate the grandeur of this once-spectacular monument.

a. *The Ruins*

The remaining columns and pieces provide a glimpse of the temple's previous splendor. You can see the base and the lowest sections of the columns, which were created using white marble. Admire the beautiful carvings and architectural elements that have endured the test of time.

b. *The Cult Statue*

Inside the temple, there stood a beautiful cult figure of Artemis, carved by the famed Greek sculptor Phidias. Unfortunately, the statue is no longer there, but historical documents describe it as a masterwork constructed of gold and ebony.

c. *The Ephesus Archaeological Site*

While you're in the region, don't miss the opportunity to tour the greater Ephesus Archaeological Site. It is home to several other historic monuments, including the Library of Celsus, the Great Theatre, and the Terrace Houses, presenting a full glimpse of life in antiquity.

6. **Tips for Visitors**

Wear good walking shoes, since the location needs a significant amount of walking over difficult terrain.

Bring sun protection, particularly during the hot summer months, since there is minimal cover.

Stay hydrated and take a water bottle with you.

Respect the place and its historical value by avoiding touching or removing any items.

Consider hiring a qualified tour guide to acquire a greater grasp of the temple's history and the adjacent archaeological site.

Bruce Terry

CHAPTER 4

OTHER HISTORICAL SITES IN THE SURROUNDING AREA

• THE HOUSE OF THE VIRGIN MARY

1. **The House of the Virgin Mary**

The House of the Virgin Mary is an important religious and historical landmark situated near the ancient city of Ephesus in Turkey. According to Christian belief, this is thought to be the dwelling where the Virgin Mary, the mother of Jesus, spent her last years. It has become a renowned pilgrimage place for Christians and an important attraction for visitors visiting Ephesus. In this travel guide, we will cover the history, importance, and practical information for visiting the House of the Virgin Mary.

2. **Historical Background**

The history of the House of the Virgin Mary is strongly established in the Christian tradition. According to the belief, following the crucifixion of Jesus Christ, St. John the Evangelist transported Mary to Ephesus to safeguard her from persecution.

The home, which is today known as the home of the Virgin Mary, is believed to be where Mary dwelt until her Assumption into Heaven.

Bruce Terry

3. Significance

The House of the Virgin Mary carries enormous importance for Christians worldwide. It is regarded as a holy site and has been acknowledged by the Roman Catholic Church as a sacred destination of pilgrimage. The site receives thousands of tourists each year, both devout Christians and inquisitive foreigners intrigued by its historical and theological importance.

4. Location and Accessibility

The House of the Virgin Mary is situated roughly 9 kilometers (5.5 miles) from the historic city of Ephesus in Turkey. It is located atop Mount Koressos, also known as Bülbüldağı, which overlooks the Aegean Sea. The site's secluded position contributes to its spiritual aura and peacefulness.

How to Reach:

By Air: The closest major airport is Izmir Adnan Menderes Airport, situated around 80 kilometers (50 miles) from Ephesus. From the airport, you may take a cab or rent a vehicle to visit the House of the Virgin Mary.

By Car: If you're already in Turkey, you may drive to Ephesus via the well-connected road networks. From Ephesus, follow the signs to the House of the Virgin Mary.

By Public Transport: Regular buses and dolmuş (shared taxis) travel from Ephesus to the House of the Virgin Mary. They are inexpensive and a handy alternative for tourists.

5. **Visiting the House of the Virgin Mary Opening Hours:**

The House of the Virgin Mary is available to tourists year-round. The normal opening hours are from 8:00 AM to 7:00 PM during the summer months (April to October) and from 8:00 AM to 5:00 PM during the winter months (November to March). However, it's crucial to check the current operating hours before your visit, since they can be subject to change.

Admission cost: There is a nominal admission cost to see the facility. The money is utilized for the protection and management of the historical site.

Dress Code and Etiquette: As the House of the Virgin Mary is a religious place, visitors are asked to dress modestly and politely. It is recommended to wear clothes that cover the shoulders and knees. Additionally, keep a calm and respectful approach when within the home and the surrounding surroundings.

Exploring the Site: The building of the Virgin Mary comprises a basic stone building with a little church erected on top of it. The inside of the home is not extremely extravagant but has a quiet and pleasant vibe. Visitors may go around the chambers and observe where it is claimed that Mary spent her time.

7. Tips for Visitors

Visit early in the day or later in the afternoon to avoid crowds and enjoy a more serene experience.

Wear appropriate shoes since you may need to walk over difficult terrain to tour the site.

Bring water and food, particularly during the hot summer months.

Respect the sacred importance of the location and the calm of its surroundings.

• THE BASILICA OF ST. JOHN

1. **History:** The Basilica of St. John bears tremendous historical and theological value. It was erected in the 6th century AD by the Byzantine Emperor Justinian I on the purported burial location of St. John the Apostle, one of the twelve apostles of Jesus Christ. St. John is widely thought to have authored the Gospel of John, the Book of Revelation, and three Epistles. His relationship with Ephesus led to the creation of this beautiful basilica as a memorial to his life and teachings.

2. **Architecture:** The Basilica of St. John displays an excellent architectural design that exhibits the grandeur of Byzantine architecture. Although the basilica has undergone countless restorations throughout the years, it nevertheless gives visitors a sense of its past magnificence. The original construction was a cruciform church with a central dome, evocative of the Hagia Sophia in Istanbul. The basilica had a timber roof, but it was regrettably destroyed by arson in the 7th century AD.

Today, the remains of the basilica display the contours of the nave, transept, and apse. The huge central dome and portions of the walls have remained, enabling visitors to appreciate the majesty and beauty of the ancient complex. The outside is embellished with elaborately carved sculptures and reliefs, showing the creative brilliance of the Byzantine period.

3. **How to Get There**: The Basilica of St. John is situated near the historic city of Ephesus in Selçuk, Izmir Province, Turkey. If you are traveling to Turkey, the closest international airport is Izmir Adnan Menderes Airport. From the airport, you may take a cab or utilize public transit to reach Selçuk, which is around a 1-hour drive away.

Once you are in Selçuk, you can easily approach the Basilica of St. John either by walking or by a short taxi ride from the town center. The basilica is within walking distance from other prominent sights

Bruce Terry

in the region, such as the Ephesus Archaeological Site and the Temple of Artemis.

4. **What to Expect during Your Visit:** When visiting the Basilica of St. John, be ready to immerse yourself in history and spirituality. The location is both a historical landmark and a pilgrimage destination, so anticipate a mix of tourists and religious people.

Upon entering the basilica grounds, you'll be welcomed by the stunning remains of the old church. As you tour the site, you'll encounter interpretive signage giving insights into the history and importance of the basilica. It is a good idea to hire a professional guide or utilize an audio tour to acquire a more in-depth knowledge of the site's historical background.

While the Basilica of St. John is not as well-preserved as some other ancient buildings in Turkey, its historical and theological significance make it a must-visit for history aficionados and anyone interested in early Christianity.

5. **Local sites:** After you visit the Basilica of St. John, try visiting additional local sites in the region:

Ephesus Archaeological Site: One of the best-preserved ancient towns in the world, Ephesus offers well-preserved monuments such as the Library of Celsus, the Great Theatre, and the Temple of Hadrian.

Bruce Terry

Temple of Artemis: Just a short distance from the basilica, you'll discover the remains of the Temple of Artemis, one of the Seven Wonders of the Ancient World.

Home of the Virgin Mary: According to legend, this home was the last dwelling of the Virgin Mary. It is a renowned pilgrimage location for Christians and a tranquil area for introspection.

• THE EPHESUS ARCHAEOLOGICAL MUSEUMS

1. History of Ephesus

Before entering the museum, it's necessary to appreciate the historical importance of Ephesus. Originally formed as an Ionian Greek city in the 10th century BCE, Ephesus prospered under different civilizations, including the Romans and Byzantines. It became a significant economic and cultural powerhouse, famed for its majestic architecture, library, and Temple of Artemis, one of the Seven Wonders of the Ancient World.

2. The Ephesus Archaeological Museum

2.1 Location and Opening Hours

The Ephesus Archaeological Museum is located in the village of Selçuk, roughly 3 kilometers (1.8 miles) away from the ancient city of Ephesus. The museum is available to the public from [insert

Bruce Terry

opening hours] and is closed on [insert closure days]. It is essential to check the museum's website or call them in advance to confirm the working hours.

2.2 *Exhibits and Collections*

The museum exhibits an amazing collection of items discovered from Ephesus and its surrounds, spanning over many millennia. The displays are grouped chronologically, enabling visitors to observe the history of the city and its residents through time.

2.3 *Highlights*

Statue of Artemis: **Admire a partial reproduction of the famed statue of the Greek goddess Artemis, originally located in the Temple of Artemis.**

Tomb of Heracles: **View the spectacular coffin dedicated to the mythological hero Heracles, embellished with elaborate carvings.**

Fountain of Pollio: **Explore the vestiges of an old Roman fountain embellished with beautiful sculptures.**

The Ephesus Market Gate: **Witness the spectacular façade of the market gate, containing superb reliefs.**

3. **Visiting Ephesus**

3.1 *Location and How to Get There*

Ephesus itself is a short distance away from the Ephesus Archaeological Museum. Visitors may reach Ephesus via automobile, taxi, or local buses from Selçuk. If you prefer a guided tour, numerous tour companies provide day tours to Ephesus, including visits to the museum.

3.2 *Exploring the Ancient City of Ephesus*

Upon arriving at Ephesus, expect to be amazed by the wonderfully preserved ruins of this once-mighty metropolis. Highlights of the site include:

Celsus Library: A landmark edifice recognized for its magnificent exterior and duty as a storehouse of ancient wisdom.

The Great Theater: Experience the grandeur of this well-preserved Roman Theater, where great events and plays took place.

The Terrace Residences: These well-preserved residences provide a look into the everyday lives of the rich citizens of Ephesus.

The Temple of Hadrian: Admire the elaborate reliefs and friezes that decorate this Roman temple.

Bruce Terry

3.3 Practical Tips

Comfortable Footwear: Wear comfortable shoes since the old city's landscape might be rough and mountainous.

Sun Protection: Bring sunscreen, a hat, and sunglasses, since Ephesus can be sweltering during summer months.

Water and Snacks: Carry a refillable water bottle and some snacks to remain hydrated and energetic throughout your excursion.

CHAPTER 5

ACCOMMODATION OPTIONS IN EPHESUS

• LUXURY HOTELS AND RESORTS

1. **Ephesus Palace**

Overview: Ephesus Palace is a five-star luxury hotel located in the center of Selcuk, only minutes away from the ancient ruins of Ephesus. The hotel's building emanates a blend of contemporary elegance and Ottoman charm, located among beautiful gardens and breathtaking views of the Aegean Sea.

Features:

Lavish suites and rooms decorated with upmarket amenities and trendy design.

A world-class spa providing a choice of luxurious treatments and therapies.

Fine-dining restaurants present a delightful selection of Turkish and foreign cuisines.

An infinity pool with a wonderful background of the ancient Ephesus ruins.

Personalized guided tours of Ephesus and neighboring historical sites.

Bruce Terry

2. Temple of Artemis Hotel & Spa

Overview: Named after the ancient Temple of Artemis, one of the Seven Wonders of the Ancient World, this luxurious hotel provides a perfect combination of history and magnificence. Located in Selcuk, it provides an ideal location for experiencing Ephesus and the adjacent attractions.

Features:

Opulent apartments and villas with their balconies or patios overlooking the Temple of Artemis.

A magnificent spa featuring traditional Turkish hammams and a broad choice of treatments.

Fine-dining restaurants deliver gourmet cuisine produced using locally-sourced ingredients.

A rooftop bar with amazing sunset views over the Temple of Artemis.

Personalized trips to historical places and Ephesus Archaeological Museum.

3. **Aegean Riviera Resort**

Overview: Nestled on the picturesque Pamucak Beach, the Aegean Riviera Resort provides a unique beachfront experience for premium tourists seeking quiet and leisure. The resort features contemporary architecture with a hint of Turkish flare.

Features:

Lavishly equipped rooms and suites with balconies give spectacular sea or garden views.

Multiple swimming pools, including infinity pools and private cabanas.

A private beach area with loungers, beachfront restaurants, and water sports amenities.

A world-class golf course for golf aficionados.

Gourmet restaurants and pubs with an emphasis on Mediterranean food.

4. The Grand Ephesus Hotel

Overview: Situated on a hill in Selcuk, The Grand Ephesus Hotel offers a magnificent hideaway with panoramic perspectives of the town and the surrounding surroundings. Its modern architecture and excellent facilities make it a favorite option for discriminating guests.

Bruce Terry

Features:

Spacious and attractively appointed rooms and suites with contemporary amenities.

An outdoor pool with a deck overlooking the beautiful splendor of Ephesus.

A well-equipped exercise facility and a peaceful spa for refreshment.

On-site eating choices featuring a mix of Turkish and foreign delicacies.

Complimentary shuttle service to the Ephesus archaeological site.

5. **Ephesus Lodge**

Overview: For tourists seeking an intimate and unique experience, Ephesus Lodge is a boutique luxury hotel set between olive trees and fruit orchards, giving a quiet hideaway only minutes away from Ephesus.

Features:

Luxurious and distinctively built apartments with their own patios and garden views.

A nice sitting room with a fireplace for relaxing.

Bruce Terry

Fresh and locally-sourced gourmet meals are offered in the on-site restaurant.

Guided nature hikes and trips to discover the local area.

Personalized services, including private transportation and personalized itineraries.

6. **The Ottoman Ephesus**

Overview: Housed in a painstakingly restored Ottoman-era home, The Ottoman Ephesus provides a unique luxury experience, mixing history with contemporary comfort. The hotel is situated in the lovely village of Sirince, near Ephesus.

Features:

Elegant rooms and suites furnished with traditional Turkish design and contemporary facilities.

A lovely courtyard and garden create a calm ambiance.

Turkish culinary workshops and wine tastings to delight in local cuisine.

Nearby cultural and historical sites are St. John's Basilica and Isa Bey Mosque.

Personalized services, including personalized excursions and airport shuttles.

Bruce Terry

• COZY BED AND BREAKFAST

1. The Enchanted Olive Tree B&B:

Location: Nestled within beautiful olive trees, only a short drive from Ephesus, The Enchanted Olive Tree B&B provides a quiet getaway from the frenetic city life.

Features: The B&B features well-appointed rooms with traditional Turkish designs, and each room overlooks the gorgeous garden. Guests may enjoy a delightful Turkish breakfast with organic vegetables produced from their orchards. The proprietors are courteous and informed, giving good insights into the region's history and culture.

2. Historic Charm Inn: Location:

Situated in the center of Selçuk, the town closest to Ephesus, the Historic Charm Inn gives convenient access to the ancient ruins and other local attractions.

Features: This bed and breakfast is set in a renovated Ottoman-era structure, oozing beauty and elegance. The rooms are attractively designed, integrating contemporary facilities with historical accents. Guests may experience a wonderful breakfast comprising handmade jams and regional specialties. The innkeepers are enthusiastic about Ephesus' history and can organize individual guided excursions for an in-depth experience.

Bruce Terry

3. **Garden Oasis B&B:**

Location: Tucked away in a secluded area, Garden Oasis B&B is an excellent getaway for nature lovers and those seeking leisure.

Boasts: The B&B boasts a magnificent garden decorated with colorful flowers and fruit trees, offering a refreshing environment. The well-appointed rooms provide comfort and solitude, and some have individual balconies with magnificent views of the surrounding countryside. Guests may start their day with a hearty breakfast provided in the garden. The hosts are recognized for their friendly hospitality and may recommend off-the-beaten-path locations to visit.

4. **Morning Terrace Inn:**

Location: Perched on a hillside overlooking the Aegean Sea, Sunrise Terrace Inn provides spectacular morning views and a tranquil ambiance.

Features: The inn's large rooms are intended to create a pleasant and domestic atmosphere, and each room has its terrace to enjoy the lovely surroundings. Guests may enjoy a superb breakfast served on the patio, containing locally produced products. The proprietors are attentive and can plan events like cooking workshops and traditional Turkish music evenings.

5. Authentic Stone House Retreat:

Location: This delightful bed and breakfast are nestled in the ancient hamlet of Şirince, a short distance from Ephesus, noted for its cobblestone alleys and picturesque environment.

Features: The Authentic Stone House Retreat provides a unique experience with its well-preserved stone building and rustic décor. The apartments are furnished with traditional Turkish carpets and antique furnishings. Guests may have a cooked breakfast including regional specialties. The hosts are concerned about maintaining local customs and may offer cultural programs for interested tourists.

6. Seaside Serenity B&B:

Location: For those wanting a seaside experience near Ephesus, Seaside Serenity B&B is situated in the lovely hamlet of Kuşadası, noted for its stunning beaches.

Features: The B&B provides pleasant rooms with a seaside flair, and some rooms offer sea views from private balconies. Guests may relish a substantial breakfast while enjoying the coastal wind. The hosts are informed about the area's nautical history and can arrange boat expeditions to adjacent islands and secret coves.

Bruce Terry

• BOUTIQUE HOTELS WITH LOCAL CHARM

1. Understanding Boutique Hotels in Ephesus

Boutique hotels are tiny, intimate facilities that pride themselves on delivering customized services and a distinct ambiance. Unlike huge chain hotels, boutique hotels give a feeling of location, frequently reflecting the local culture and history in their architecture, design, and culinary offerings. Ephesus boasts a superb range of boutique hotels that pay tribute to the region's antiquity while giving all the conveniences contemporary guests demand.

2. Top Boutique Hotels in Ephesus

a. *The Ottoman House Boutique Hotel:* Located in the center of Selcuk, a lovely town near Ephesus, The Ottoman House Boutique Hotel is a renovated Ottoman-era palace. The hotel oozes real Turkish beauty with its timber building, oriental carpets, and Turkish artwork. Each room is beautifully furnished, and the courtyard provides a calm place to rest. Don't miss the traditional Turkish breakfast offered here, highlighting local delights.

b. *Ephesus Terrace Boutique Hotel:* Offering stunning views of the ancient Ephesus ruins, this boutique hotel is a mix of modern luxury and traditional touches. The rooms are large and well-appointed, providing modern comforts with Turkish influences. The hotel's rooftop patio is a feature, where you can enjoy spectacular sunsets over the ancient landscape.

c. *Saint John Hotel:* Situated in the quiet town of Sirince, a short drive from Ephesus, Saint John Hotel embraces the area's rustic charm. The hotel's stone building, hardwood furniture, and picturesque surroundings give a lovely getaway from the hectic world. Guests may indulge in local wine sampling and traditional Turkish cuisine at the hotel's restaurant.

3. Experiencing Local Culture

One of the key benefits of staying at boutique hotels is their attention to maintaining local culture. In Ephesus, these hotels typically engage with neighborhood artists and craftsmen to present traditional artwork, fabrics, and handicrafts. Some hotels may even provide workshops where visitors may partake in activities like pottery making, carpet weaving, or traditional culinary lessons, providing an entire cultural experience.

4. Culinary Delights

The boutique hotels in Ephesus take great pleasure in their gastronomic offerings. Many of them feature on-site restaurants providing traditional Turkish cuisine produced from locally sourced ingredients. From juicy kebabs to delicious mezes and scented

Turkish coffee, you'll have the chance to experience genuine delicacies right at your hotel.

5. **Exploring the Ancient City of Ephesus**

Staying at a boutique hotel in Ephesus puts you near the awe-inspiring ancient city. Wake up early to beat the crowds and tour the well-preserved remains of Ephesus, including the Celsus Library, the Great Theater, and the Temple of Artemis. Guided tours are provided for more in-depth knowledge of the historical importance of these ancient monuments.

Bruce Terry

EPHESUS TRAVEL GUIDE 2023-2024

CHAPTER 6
LOCAL CUISINES AND DINING
• TRADITIONAL TURKISH DISHES

1. **Turkish Breakfast (Kahvaltı):** Start your day like a native with a classic Turkish breakfast. Kahvaltı often consists of a spread of several meals, including olives, cheeses (such as beyaz peynir and kaşar), cucumbers, tomatoes, and fresh bread. Menemen, a delectable egg dish cooked with tomatoes, peppers, and spices, is a must-try. Don't forget to indulge in the sweet side of breakfast with honey, jam, and pastries like börek or simit.

2. **Köfte:** Köfte, or Turkish meatballs, are an integral feature of Turkish cuisine. These luscious minced meat patties, generally prepared from lamb, beef, or a mix of both, are seasoned with a blend of fragrant herbs and spices. They are generally served with a side of grilled veggies, rice, and a crisp salad.

3. **Kebabs:** Turkish kebabs are recognized internationally, and Ephesus provides a diversity of selections. Some popular kebabs you should taste include:

Shish Kebab: Cubes of marinated meat (typically lamb or chicken) are skewered and cooked to perfection. Served with rice and a fresh salad.

Döner Kebab: Thinly cut slices of seasoned meat (lamb, cattle, or chicken) are grilled on a vertical rotisserie. The meat is shaved off and commonly served in a wrap or with rice and salads.

4. **Mezes:** Mezes are appetizers that display the tremendous diversity of tastes in Turkish cuisine. When in Ephesus, make sure to taste some classic mezes, such as:

Hummus: A combination of chickpeas, tahini, lemon, and garlic, drizzled with olive oil and served with pita bread.

Cacık: A delicious yogurt-based dip with cucumber, mint, garlic, and olive oil.

Patlıcan Ezmesi: Roasted eggplant blended with tomatoes, peppers, olive oil, and numerous seasonings.

5. **Pide:** Pide is commonly referred to as "Turkish pizza." It's a boat-shaped flatbread topped with different toppings. Some common toppings include minced beef, cheese, spinach, and sucuk (Turkish sausage). Pide is best consumed hot and fresh from the oven.

6. **Baklava:** No Turkish gastronomic journey is complete without indulging in some Baklava. This delightful pastry is comprised of layers of filo dough filled with chopped nuts (typically pistachios, walnuts, or almonds) and soaked in sweet syrup or honey. The mix of flaky pastry and nutty sweetness is enticing.

7. **Turkish Delight (Lokum):** Lokum, commonly known as Turkish delight, is a confection made from flour, sugar, and flavorings like rosewater, citrus, or nuts. It comes in numerous colors and tastes, making it a pleasant treat to satiate your sweet craving.

8. **Çay (Turkish Tea) and Kahve (Turkish coffee):** Turkish tea (çay) and coffee (kahve) are fundamental drinks in Turkish culture. Sip on some black tea offered in little tulip-shaped cups or experience the rich flavors of Turkish coffee, which is often served with a glass of water.

MUST-TRY RESTAURANTS IN EPHESUS

1. **Artemis Restaurant & Meyhane:** Located near the ancient ruins of Ephesus, Artemis Restaurant & Meyhane is a popular venue that provides a wonderful combination of traditional Turkish food and a vibrant ambiance. Here, you may taste a large choice of mezes (small meals), grilled kebabs, and fresh fish. Don't miss their luscious lamb dishes, such as "Kuzu Tandır" (slow-cooked lamb) and "Kuzu Şiş" (grilled lamb skewers). The restaurant's great welcome and live music performances add to the overall attractiveness.

2. **Antique Terrace Restaurant:** Situated on a scenic hill above the historic city, Antique Terrace Restaurant provides not only scrumptious meals but also spectacular vistas. This restaurant

focuses on genuine Turkish cuisine produced using locally obtained ingredients. Their "Testi Kebabı," a slow-cooked pork stew served in a clay pot, is a must-try meal. Additionally, the restaurant's balcony offers a fantastic environment for a romantic supper at sunset.

3. **Ejder Restaurant:** If you're seeking to indulge in a magnificent seafood feast, Ejder Restaurant is the place to go. Located near the waterfront, this restaurant delivers an outstanding assortment of freshly caught fish and seafood meals. Their "Karides Güveç" (shrimp casserole) and "Levrek Izgara" (grilled sea bass) are highly regarded. The pleasant personnel and the peaceful ambiance offer a great eating experience.

4. **Sipahi Restaurant:** For an excellent dining experience with a dash of contemporary, Sipahi Restaurant stands out as a great pick. The restaurant's trendy design and unique cuisine make it popular among residents and visitors alike. You may experience Turkish classics with a twist, such as "Mantı with Yogurt Foam" (a unique variation of Turkish dumplings) or "Baklava Ice Cream" for dessert. This is a terrific spot to discover the combination of classic and modern cuisines.

5. **Selçuk Koftecisi:** No vacation to Turkey is complete without sampling "köfte," the famed Turkish meatballs, and Selçuk Koftecisi is recognized for offering some of the finest in the area.

This small café, nestled in the center of Selçuk, provides delectable köfte prepared from a secret family recipe. Pair your köfte with traditional Turkish sides like "piyaz" (white bean salad) and "ezme" (spicy tomato and pepper dip) for a genuine flavor of local cuisine.

6. **Café La Vie:** If you're in the mood for a relaxing café environment, Café La Vie in Selçuk is an ideal option. This beautiful café provides a broad variety of foreign foods with Turkish classics. Whether you're seeking a substantial breakfast, a fresh salad, or a handmade burger, Café La Vie offers something to fulfill every need. Don't forget to taste their range of Turkish sweets, including "Künefe" and "Sütlaç."

7. **Sirince Garden Restaurant:** A short drive from Ephesus, the hamlet of Şirince is noted for its picturesque beauty and charming ambiance. While touring this charming town, make sure to visit Sirince Garden Restaurant, hidden between orchards and vineyards. The restaurant provides a farm-to-table experience with organic products and serves delectable Turkish favorites. Enjoy your dinner in the calm garden environment, away from the noise and bustle.

Bruce Terry

Bruce Terry

CHAPTER 7

OUTDOOR ACTIVITIES AND EXCURSIONS

• HIKING AND NATURE WALKS

1. Why Choose Hiking and Nature Walks in Ephesus?

Ephesus' natural beauty and historical importance combine to offer a unique and intriguing location for trekking and nature hikes. By opting to explore the outdoors, tourists may have a more personal relationship with the region's history and present, away from the throngs at the archaeological sites. The following sections highlight some of the primary reasons why hiking in Ephesus is a must-do activity:

a. *Tranquil Escapes*

Hiking and nature hikes provide a tranquil getaway from the hectic tourist districts of Ephesus. The serene environment and stunning surroundings enable tourists to connect with nature and discover moments of tranquillity.

Bruce Terry

b. *Cultural and Historical Connection*

Many of the hiking paths in Ephesus traverse past ancient ruins, historic monuments, and traditional villages, giving hikers a fuller knowledge of the region's cultural history and historical importance.

c. *Diverse Landscapes*

Ephesus features different settings, from lush woods and rolling hills to rivers and gorges. Each route gives a unique chance to observe the area's natural treasures up close.

d. *Wildlife and Flora*

Nature aficionados will enjoy the opportunity to see a range of animal species and experience the region's unique vegetation, including indigenous plants and wildflowers.

2. Top Hiking and Nature Walk Trails in Ephesus

Ephesus provides various well-maintained routes that appeal to hikers of all ability levels. Below are some of the excellent paths worth exploring:

Bruce Terry

a. *Kestel to Cave of the Seven Sleepers*

This fairly tough trek carries hikers through lovely olive gardens and deep pine woods. The centerpiece of the trip is the Cave of the Seven Sleepers, a mythical place recorded in religious literature.

b. *Mount Bülbül*

For more experienced hikers seeking a gratifying challenge, Mount Bülbül is a wonderful option. The peak rewards climbers with breathtaking panoramic views of Ephesus and the Aegean shoreline.

c. *Güvercinada Peninsula Trail*

This coastline route provides a very simple trek, excellent for families and unhurried adventurers. The trail meanders over the peninsula, passing by old walls and affording spectacular panoramas of the sea.

d. *Kaystros River Trail*

Perfect for nature aficionados, this walk follows the flowing Kaystros River, allowing an opportunity to watch local wildlife and rich greenery.

3. **Hiking Tips and Safety**

Before beginning a trekking experience in Ephesus, it's vital to keep the following guidelines in mind:

Bruce Terry

a. *Check Weather Conditions*

Always check the weather forecast before starting, since conditions may change swiftly in hilly places.

b. *Wear Appropriate Gear*

Ensure you wear comfortable, durable hiking shoes and proper attire for the season. Don't forget to bring a hat, sunglasses, and sunscreen for sun protection.

c. Stay Hydrated and Bring Snacks

Carry an extra supply of water and energy-boosting foods to keep you fuelled throughout the journey.

d. *Respect Nature and Historic Sites*

Leave no trace behind and respect the natural environment and historical monuments you meet.

e. *Consider a Guided Tour*

For those unfamiliar with the area or wanting more in-depth understanding, hiring a local guide may improve the hiking experience and give vital insights into the region's history and culture.

Bruce Terry

• BOAT TOURS ALONG THE AEGEAN COAST

I. Boat Tour Options

Traditional Wooden Gulet Cruises: Gulets are historic wooden boats, frequently embellished with beautiful carvings and sails, bringing a sense of authenticity and elegance to the boat trip experience. These cruises normally vary from half-day to full-day excursions, giving a combination of relaxation, swimming chances, and visits to adjacent islands and hidden coves.

Speedboat Adventures: For thrill-seekers, speedboat cruises are a wonderful alternative. These trips provide a faster-paced experience, enabling passengers to cover more territory and explore farther down the coastline. Speedboat trips typically include stops at secluded beaches, snorkeling areas, and adventurous water sports.

Private boat Charters: For an opulent and customized experience, travelers may choose private boat charters. Private charters provide exclusivity, flexibility, and the ability to construct a personalized itinerary according to your tastes, making them great for special events or private groups.

II. **Highlights of Boat Tours Pamucak Beach:** Starting your boat excursion from Ephesus, Pamucak Beach is frequently the first stop. With its golden beaches and clean waves, this beach gives a superb chance for swimming and relaxing.

Kusadasi Peninsula: The boat cruises normally follow the magnificent coastline, going by the Kusadasi Peninsula, where you may see majestic cliffs, rich flora, and attractive coastal towns.

Dilek National Park: Many boat cruises include a stop at Dilek National Park, commonly known as Milli Park. This protected region provides a pure natural setting, suitable for trekking, animal watching, and connecting with nature.

Güvercinada Castle: Some boat cruises take you to Güvercinada Castle, a magnificent medieval fortification built on a tiny island close off the shore. The castle provides magnificent views of the surrounding sea and shoreline.

Claros Island: If your boat excursion involves an additional itinerary, you could visit Claros Island, an ancient holy place noted for its Temple of Apollo and Oracle.

III. **Practical Tips for Boat Tours**

Booking in Advance: Boat cruises may be popular, particularly during busy tourist seasons. It's essential to reserve your trip in advance to ensure your position and prevent disappointment.

Pack basics: Don't forget to carry basics such as sunscreen, a hat, sunglasses, a towel, and a camera to record the lovely view.

Comfortable clothes: Wear light, comfortable clothes and footwear suited for boat travel and possibly aquatic sports.

Motion Sickness: If you are prone to motion sickness, consider taking motion sickness medicine before the trip.

Respect the Environment: During your boat trip, be careful of the environment. Avoid leaving any rubbish behind and follow principles for responsible travel.

IV. Safety Precautions

Listen to the Crew: Pay attention to safety briefings offered by the boat crew, including information regarding life jackets and emergency procedures.

Remain Hydrated: It may become hot on boat trips, so remain hydrated by drinking lots of water.

Swimming Safety: If you intend to swim during stops, verify you are a competent swimmer and stick to the safety precautions supplied by the crew.

Weather Conditions: Boat cruises are subject to weather conditions. In case of poor weather, the excursion can be postponed or canceled for safety reasons.

Bruce Terry

• EXPLORING THE ANCIENT CITY OF PRIENE

1. Historical Background

Discover the beginnings of Priene, which goes back to the 4th century BC. Learn about its importance as one of the 12 Ionian cities and its strategic position on the steep slopes of Mount Mycale overlooking the Aegean Sea.

Understand the cultural and historical backdrop of Priene, including its government, architecture, and prominent personalities who affected its evolution throughout the years.

2. Getting There

Explore the transportation alternatives accessible to reach Priene. Whether you're coming by flight, rail, or automobile, we give extensive recommendations on the best routes to take.

Discover adjacent towns or cities where you may locate lodging, like Kusadasi or Selcuk, which are popular bases for touring the Ephesus area.

3. Planning Your Visit

Seasonal considerations: Learn about the ideal time to visit Priene to avoid adverse weather conditions and excessive people.

Bruce Terry

Entrance fees and operational hours: Get information about the current admission costs and opening hours of the archaeological site.

Guided tours: Consider the advantages of hiring a qualified guide to deepen your awareness of Priene's history and architecture.

4. Exploring Priene

4.1 *The Temple of Athena*

Delve into the history and importance of the Temple of Athena, one of Priene's most renowned temples. Learn about its distinctive design and architectural characteristics.

Discover the religious activities and ceremonies that took place in the temple, devoted to the goddess Athena, the defender of the city.

4.2 *Prytaneion and Bouleuterion*

Explore the Prytaneion, the administrative heart of Priene, and discover its importance in civic life.

Visit the Bouleuterion, where the municipal council conducted meetings and made crucial decisions for the town.

4.3 *The Theater*

Uncover the splendor of the old theater at Priene, which previously held dramatic plays and public meetings.

Bruce Terry

Learn about its acoustics and technical wonders that enabled thousands of people to enjoy the concerts.

4.4 *The Agora*

Walk through Agora, the hub of the city's social and commercial life. Understand its layout and the sorts of activities that took place there.

Discover the sculptures and monuments that graced the Agora and the tales they tell about Priene's history.

4.5 *The Houses of Priene*

Learn about the residential architecture in Priene by visiting the well-preserved residences. Understand the lifestyle of the ancient people and their creative interests.

Explore the House of Alexander the Great and other noteworthy houses that give insights into the city's social structure.

5. Practical Tips

Wear comfortable attire and sturdy footwear ideal for walking over rough terrain.

Stay hydrated, particularly during the hot summer months, by carrying a water bottle.

Bruce Terry

To protect yourself from the sun, pack a hat, sunscreen, and sunglasses.

Respect the ancient site by avoiding climbing on the ruins or touching sensitive structures.

Carry a camera to record the amazing scenery and experiences throughout your stay.

Bruce Terry

EPHESUS TRAVEL GUIDE 2023-2024

CHAPTER 8

SHOPPING IN EPHESUS

• LOCAL HANDICRAFTS AND SOUVENIRS

1. **Understanding Ephesian Handcrafts:** Ephesus has a long-standing legacy of talented craftsmen who have mastered diverse skills handed down through generations. Some of the major handcrafts you might discover here include:

a. *Carpets & Kilims:* Ephesian carpets and kilims are recognized worldwide for their elaborate patterns, brilliant colors, and superb workmanship. Witness the weaving process at local workshops and uncover the creativity behind making these wonderful fabrics.

b. *Pottery:* The region is known for its terracotta pottery, which holds deep links to its ancient history. From modest containers to intricate ornamental pieces, Ephesian pottery exhibits a combination of classic and modern themes.

c. *Leather Goods:* Ephesus provides a varied assortment of leather items, including purses, coats, shoes, and accessories. Look for high-quality, locally-made leather products that exhibit excellent workmanship.

d. *Jewelry:* Discover unique jewelry pieces that embody Ephesian aesthetics, incorporating components influenced by antique themes and modern styles.

2. **Exploring Local Souvenirs:** In addition to handcrafts, Ephesus provides a fascinating choice of souvenirs that embody the character of the area. As you browse around markets and stores, keep a look out for these delightful mementos:

a. *Evil Eye Talismans:* The evil eye talisman, known as "Nazar Boncugu" in Turkish, is a prominent symbol thought to guard against bad energy and offer good luck. These blue glass beads are a popular memento option.

b. *Turkish pleasure:* Treat your taste buds to the exquisite tastes of Turkish pleasure, or "lokum." These delicious, chewy confections come in a variety of flavors and are elegantly packed, making them great presents for loved ones back home.

c. *Olive Oil Products:* Ephesus is located in the center of Turkey's olive oil-producing zone. Look for excellent olive oil and olive oil-based skincare products, including soaps and lotions.

d. *Handmade Ceramics:* Apart from the bigger pottery objects, you may discover little, hand-painted ceramic pieces like ornamental tiles, bowls, and plates that make for lovely and utilitarian gifts.

3. *Best Places to Shop:* Make the most of your souvenir searching experience by visiting these suggested shopping sites in Ephesus:

a. *Kemeraltı Bazaar:* Located in Izmir, Kemeraltı is one of the oldest and biggest bazaars in the area. Here, you may discover a comprehensive assortment of handcrafts, souvenirs, spices, and more.

b. *Local Workshops:* Visit the workshops of local artists to observe their handiwork firsthand and acquire original, one-of-a-kind artifacts.

c. *Selçuk Market:* This weekly market in Selçuk, near Ephesus, provides a superb choice of souvenirs, fresh vegetables, and local items.

d. *Boutique Boutiques:* Explore the boutique boutiques spread around Ephesus, where you may discover selected collections of high-quality handcrafts and souvenirs.

4. *Ethical Shopping and Supporting Local Craftsmen:* When shopping for handcrafts and souvenirs, consider supporting local craftsmen and sustainable methods. Seek for Fair Trade businesses or cooperatives that provide fair salaries and working conditions for the craftspeople.

Bruce Terry

• EPHESUS' STREET MARKETS

1. **The Grand Bazaar of Ephesus:** This ancient market goes back to the 1st century AD and functioned as a prominent commerce hub in antiquity. Today, it continues to be a hive of activity, bringing both residents and visitors. As you wander the cobblestone alleyways, you'll discover an assortment of stores offering traditional Turkish handicrafts, textiles, jewelry, pottery, spices, and souvenirs. Don't forget to develop your negotiating abilities, since haggling is a widespread practice here!

2. **Arcadian Street Market:** The Arcadian Street Market, commonly known as "Harbour Street," provides a more sophisticated shopping experience compared to the Grand Bazaar. Lined with stunning old structures and stores, this street was formerly the primary avenue linking the commercial port to the city center. Today, tourists may browse through a collection of high-quality handcrafted items, including leather products, exquisite woodwork art pieces, and locally produced olive oil. Take a leisurely walk and absorb the historical ambiance while indulging in retail therapy.

3. **Curetes Street Market:** Curetes Street, an attractive marble-paved street lined by Corinthian columns and embellished with antique sculptures, is an important visit for every shopaholic. This street was mostly a residential neighborhood for rich Ephesians, but

it also featured a lively market. Nowadays, it has a variety of lovely shops and cafés, providing anything from traditional Turkish carpets and textiles to unusual artworks. The Curetes Street Market gives a wonderful chance to view Ephesus' ancient beauties while browsing for one-of-a-kind artifacts.

4. **Local Delicacies & Culinary Treasures:** Ephesus' street markets are not only about tangible products; they also give a chance to experience the region's wonderful food. Be sure to experience some of the local delights, such as "kebabs" (grilled meat), "börek" (savory pastries), "baklava" (sweet pastry with nuts and syrup), and "Turkish delight" (gelatinous confections). Many sellers provide complimentary sampling, enabling you to experience new tastes and bring back tasty keepsakes for loved ones.

5. **Tips for an Enjoyable Shopping Experience:** Bargain with a Smile: Haggling is a typical technique in Turkish marketplaces, but try to retain a polite tone during the transaction. It's all part of the experience and may lead to huge savings.

Cash is King: While bigger establishments may take credit cards, smaller merchants frequently prefer cash. Carry Turkish Lira to prevent any payment problems.

Respect Local traditions: Ephesus is a culturally rich location, therefore be aware of local traditions and dress modestly, particularly while visiting holy sites near the marketplaces.

Bruce Terry

Early Bird Advantage: To avoid crowds and have a more customized shopping experience, try visiting the markets early in the morning.

Excellent over Quantity: With so many alternatives available, take your time to choose excellent goods that genuinely connect with you or your loved ones.

• SHOPPING CENTERS AND MALLS

1. **Kusadasi Grand Bazaar Description:** The Kusadasi Grand Bazaar is one of the most famous shopping places in Ephesus. It's a lively and dynamic marketplace where travelers can immerse themselves in the local culture and locate a vast assortment of things.

What to Expect: Visitors may explore countless stores and booths offering traditional Turkish things like handmade carpets, fabrics, pottery, spices, and leather goods. The skill of negotiating is a popular practice here, so be prepared to negotiate the rates.

Tips: Remember to start with a cheaper price while bargaining and be courteous throughout the process. Also, examine the quality of things before making a purchase.

2. **Ephesus Commercial Centre Description:** Ephesus Shopping Centre is a contemporary commercial complex located near the ancient site of Ephesus. It provides a combination of traditional

Turkish items and foreign brands, giving tourists a well-rounded shopping experience.

What to Expect: The shopping complex contains a range of businesses ranging from apparel boutiques, jewelry stores, souvenir shops, and electronics merchants. It's a wonderful spot to get real Turkish treats and local wines.

Tips: Ensure you browse both the traditional Turkish boutiques and the trendy retailers to obtain the best of both worlds.

3. **Forum Shopping Center Description:** Located in Selcuk, a neighboring town to Ephesus, the Forum Shopping Center is an excellent alternative for those searching for a more leisurely shopping experience away from the tourist hordes.

What to Expect: The retail area includes a selection of businesses providing apparel, shoes, accessories, and household products. It's an amazing site to get economical and fashionable things.

Tips: Enjoy a leisurely walk around the retail area and visit the lovely streets of Selcuk thereafter.

4. **Kervan Outlet Description:** For those who appreciate inexpensive shopping, Kervan Outlet is a must-visit place in Ephesus.

Bruce Terry

What to Expect: This outlet mall provides a choice of branded items at reduced costs. From apparel to shoes, accessories to home products, Kervan Outlet delivers a budget-friendly shopping experience.

Tips: Check for seasonal specials and promotions to obtain the greatest bargains.

CHAPTER 9

EPHESUS' NIGHTLIFE AND ENTERTAINMENT

• BARS AND CLUBS

1. Understanding Ephesus Nightlife

Before getting into the individual places, it's vital to appreciate the core of Ephesus' nightlife culture. While the city possesses a rich historical legacy, its pubs and clubs represent a unique combination of traditional Turkish characteristics and current foreign influences. Expect a vibrant and cheerful environment, as residents and visitors alike join together to celebrate life and create memorable memories.

2. Best Time to Experience Ephesus Nightlife

The main tourist season in Ephesus is during the summer months (June to August), which also corresponds with the busiest period for the nightlife scene. During this week, the clubs and bars are bustling with guests, and you can anticipate events, parties, and live performances to be in full flow. If you want a more relaxing experience, try going during the shoulder seasons (spring and fall) when the weather is still great, and the crowds are more bearable.

Bruce Terry

3. Top Bars in Ephesus

a) *Terrace Bar Ephesus*

Located inside the center of Ephesus, Terrace Bar gives an unrivaled view of the historic city as the sun sets. This rooftop bar provides a vast choice of cool cocktails, local wines, and traditional Turkish beverages. The peaceful ambiance, along with exquisite mezze plates, offers an ideal location to rest after a day of touring.

b) *Boomerang Bar*

Situated on a lovely cobblestone lane, Boomerang Bar has a comfortable and friendly ambiance. With its friendly staff and a broad selection of drinks and beers, it's a wonderful venue to mix with both visitors and residents alike. Enjoy the live music performances or play a game of pool while you absorb the pleasant ambiance.

c) *Hemingway Cocktail Bar*

If you're a cocktail fan, Hemingway Cocktail Bar is a must-visit. The expert mixologists prepare both traditional and inventive drinks utilizing locally obtained ingredients. The softly lighted and contemporary decor offers a trendy environment, making it a great setting for a more expensive evening experience.

Bruce Terry

4. Top Clubs in Ephesus

a) *Club Temple*

Known for its high-energy gatherings, Club Temple is Ephesus' flagship nightclub. The amazing music system and spectacular lighting set the atmosphere for an incredible night of dancing and merriment. International DJs regularly grace the turntables, delivering a combination of electronic dance music, hip-hop, and popular songs.

b) *Aura Club Ephesus*

Located near the ancient theater, Aura Club Ephesus has a unique location, mixing historical settings with a contemporary party ambiance. The club provides themed events, like beach parties and foam parties, assuring an engaging and unforgettable night out.

5. Safety and Etiquette

While Ephesus is a generally secure site, it's always vital to take some precautions while enjoying the evening. Travel in groups, avoid wandering alone late at night and keep your possessions safe. Additionally, observe local norms and traditions, especially when it comes to clothing rules and alcohol usage.

Bruce Terry

6. Getting Around

Most of the pubs and clubs are situated within walking distance of each other in the center district of Ephesus. Taxis are easily accessible if you're staying away from the city center. If you intend to indulge in alcohol, consider employing a designated driving service or public transit.

• TRADITIONAL TURKISH MUSIC AND DANCE SHOW

1. **Ephesus:** Ephesus is an ancient city situated in the western region of Turkey, near the Aegean Sea. It was once an important hub of Greek and Roman civilization and is today a vital archaeological site and a renowned tourist attraction. Apart from its historical importance, Ephesus provides tourists an opportunity to enjoy the rich cultural legacy of Turkey via its traditional music and dance performances.

2. **Traditional Turkish Music:** Turkish music is firmly steeped in history and represents the country's numerous cultural influences. It is a combination of numerous elements from Central Asia, the Middle East, and the Mediterranean. Traditional Turkish music is distinguished by a broad variety of instruments, such as the oud (a lute-like string instrument), saz (a long-necked plucked string instrument), and the ney (an end-blown flute). The employment of

unusual scales, known as "makams," gives Turkish music its distinctive and expressive feel.

3. **Traditional Turkish Dance:** Turkish dance is a vital aspect of the country's cultural expression, and it differs across various areas. Some of the most well-known Turkish dances are the "Halay," a vibrant group dance done in rings or lines, and the "Zeybek," a solo male dance expressing valor and heroism. The "Horon" is another attractive dance form prevalent in the Black Sea area, marked by rapid and rhythmic movements.

4. **The Venue and Show Overview:** Visitors to Ephesus may experience a spectacular Traditional Turkish Music and Dance Show in numerous locations inside the city. One of the favorite sites is a typical Turkish restaurant, where the act is frequently complemented by a scrumptious Turkish supper. The concerts are often conducted in the evening to create an enticing environment with soft lighting and an inviting mood.

5. **Concert Program:** The concert generally opens with a fascinating exhibition of traditional Turkish music performed by professional musicians on different instruments. They feature a varied spectrum of melodies, each eliciting a particular feeling and atmosphere. The audience is serenaded with deep tunes and sometimes even encouraged to join in the singing.

6. **Dazzling Dance Performances:** Following the musical performance, the dance part starts, including outstanding dancers clothed in bright costumes. The dancers delicately interpret the song via their motions, exhibiting the beauty and intensity of Turkish dance genres. Spectators are drawn by the precise footwork, whirling skirts, and the general intensity of the performances.

7. **Audience Participation:** The charm of these presentations resides in their participatory aspect. After the major performances, visitors are typically urged to join the dancers on the floor to learn a few fundamental moves of Turkish dance. This engagement builds a feeling of connection with Turkish culture and produces lasting experiences for the tourists.

8. **Cultural Significance:** Attending a traditional Turkish music and dance concert at Ephesus provides guests with a rare chance to engage with the rich cultural legacy of Turkey. It enables people to experience heartfelt interpretations of the country's music and see the creative portrayal of its lively dance traditions. Through these performances, tourists receive insight into the values, customs, and tales handed down through centuries.

Bruce Terry

EVENING STROLLS AND PROMENADES

1. **Sunset at Artemis Temple:** Begin your evening trip with a visit to the remnants of the Artemis Temple, one of the Seven Wonders of the Ancient World. As the sun sets behind the columns, the atmosphere turns ethereal, giving a fantastic background for photography and moments of introspection.

2. **The Marble Street Walk:** As twilight creeps down, take a leisurely walk along the old Marble Street (Harbour Street), which originally linked the port to the city center. The mellow light of lampposts and the well-preserved ruins on each side create an environment that takes you back in time. Learn about the history of the street via educational plaques and savor the unique sensation of treading in the footsteps of ancient Ephesians.

3. **Ephesus Terrace Houses Night Tour**: Discover the grandeur of ancient Roman lives by enjoying a night tour of the Ephesus Terrace Houses. Illuminated walkways carry you through these well-preserved townhouses, allowing a look into the life of the privileged elite. Witness the amazing frescoes and mosaics that cover the walls, bringing the past to life beneath the night sky.

4. **The Grand Theater Spectacle:** As the stars glitter overhead, witness the acoustics of the world-famous Grand Theater during nighttime performances. This spectacular amphitheater, which formerly housed gladiator bouts and theatrical events, today comes

alive with cultural acts, concerts, and reenactments. Enjoy a show or just relax and absorb the ambiance of this ancient gem.

5. **Candlelit Dinner in Selçuk:** After the thrill of exploring historic Ephesus, travel to the adjacent lovely village of Selçuk for a delicious evening meal. Many nearby eateries provide traditional Turkish food served in romantic lighted gardens. Indulge in classic foods like kebabs, mezes, and baklava while savoring the warm hospitality of the people.

6. **Nightlife in Kusadasi:** If you're looking for a livelier evening, travel to the colorful seaside town of Kusadasi. Here, you'll discover a mix of pubs, clubs, and entertainment places to satisfy all preferences. Enjoy live music, dance to the newest sounds, or just relax with a beverage while watching the sea. Kusadasi's nightlife has something for everyone.

7. **Sirince Hamlet Twilight Visit:** For a unique experience, take a short excursion to the charming hamlet of Sirince during the twilight hours. The picturesque cobblestone lanes, classic buildings, and handmade businesses make a beautiful atmosphere. Savor the local fruit wines, olive oils, and handicrafts while seeing the village's metamorphosis as the sun sets.

Bruce Terry

CHAPTER 10

PRACTICAL TIPS FOR TRAVELING TO EPHESUS

• VISA AND ENTRY REQUIREMENTS

1. **Passport Validity:** First and foremost, confirm that your passport is valid for at least six months beyond your anticipated stay in Turkey. It is usual practice for many nations to require travelers to have a passport with adequate validity to prevent any possible complications during immigration procedures.

2. **Visa Requirements:** The visa requirements for Turkey vary based on your nationality and the purpose of your travel. Turkey has introduced an electronic visa (e-Visa) system that enables nationals of numerous countries to get a visa online before visiting. The e-Visa is often given for tourism, business, or transit reasons and is valid for multiple entries within a set term.

3. **Countries Eligible for e-Visa:** Turkey's e-Visa was accessible to citizens of over 100 countries, including the United States, Canada, the United Kingdom, Australia, most European Union member states, and many more. However, visa laws are subject to change, and it is necessary to check the current eligibility list on the official Republic of Turkey Electronic Visa Application System website or confer with the closest Turkish embassy or consulate.

Bruce Terry

4. **How to Apply for an e-Visa:** To apply for an e-Visa, you must visit the official website of the Republic of Turkey's Electronic Visa Application System. The application procedure is basic and mainly entails giving personal information, trip details, passport data, and paying the visa cost using a credit or debit card. After the application is reviewed and accepted, the e-Visa will be given to your email address, and you must print it off and bring it with you throughout your trip.

5. **Visa on Arrival**: For nationals of certain countries not eligible for an e-Visa, Turkey could provide a visa-on-arrival alternative. However, it is vital to verify the latest details about visa on-arrival availability, since this option could vary dependent on the country's visa laws.

6. **Visa Exemptions:** Turkey allows visa exemptions for nationals of certain countries, enabling them to visit the country for short periods without a visa. For example, residents of Schengen Area nations may remain in Turkey for up to 90 days during 180 days without a visa. Additionally, several countries have bilateral agreements with Turkey, which could exempt its residents from visa requirements for short stays.

7. **Work and Study Visas:** If you want to work or study in Turkey, various visa requirements apply, and you will need to get the proper visa from a Turkish embassy or consulate in your home country before your journey.

8. **Entry Regulations during COVID-19:** Due to the worldwide COVID-19 epidemic, travel restrictions and admission criteria may vary regularly. It is vital to verify the current travel warnings, entrance requirements, and any health and safety standards published by the Turkish government before arranging your trip to Ephesus.

HEALTH AND SAFETY PRECAUTIONS

1. **Travel Insurance:** Before you set out on your adventure, buy comprehensive travel insurance that covers medical emergencies, trip cancellations, and other unexpected circumstances. This will give you financial protection and peace of mind while your trips.

2. **Medical Check-Up:** Ensure you consult your healthcare professional before your vacation to Ephesus. A complete medical check-up can assist discover any underlying health concerns and ensure you are ready for travel. It is also a chance to update vaccines and medicines.

3. **Stay Hydrated:** The weather in Ephesus may be hot and dry, particularly during the summer months. Carry a reusable water

bottle and drink lots of water throughout the day to keep hydrated. Dehydration may lead to weariness and other health concerns, thus it is crucial to maintain sufficient water levels.

4. **Sun Protection:** Protect yourself from the sun's damaging rays by wearing sunscreen with a high SPF, a wide-brimmed hat, and sunglasses. Sunburn and heatstroke may be major health dangers, particularly in the sweltering Turkish summers.

5. **Comfortable clothes:** Wear comfortable, lightweight clothes that cover your skin to defend against the sun and mosquitoes. Proper footwear is particularly necessary since Ephesus requires a lot of walking over rough terrain.

6. **Mosquito Protection:** Ephesus is situated in a location where mosquitoes are numerous, particularly during certain periods of the year. Use insect repellent and wear long-sleeved shirts and trousers during the nights and in locations with thick vegetation.

7. **Food and Water Safety:** While Ephesus provides excellent gastronomic experiences, be wary about ingesting street food and select renowned establishments. Ensure the meal is completely prepared and prevent raw or undercooked items. Drink bottled or boiling water and avoid ice in your beverages to prevent waterborne infections.

8. **Emergency Numbers:** Save critical contact numbers, including local emergency services, your country's embassy, and your travel insurance provider, on your phone. Knowing whom to contact in case of an emergency may be useful.

9. **COVID-19 Precautions:** Check the current COVID-19 standards and travel restrictions before your journey to Ephesus. Carry masks, and hand sanitizers, and exercise social distancing as necessary. Respect any health protocols imposed by local authorities.

10. **Be Cautious at Archaeological Sites:** Ephesus is packed with ancient ruins and archaeological sites. While exploring, be careful and remain inside approved zones to prevent mishaps. Climbing on ruins or buildings is not only hazardous but may also lead to harm to historical items.

11. **Petty Crime Awareness:** Ephesus is a famous tourist site, and like any other busy area, there can be pickpockets or petty criminals. Keep your stuff safe and avoid showing precious goods publicly.

12. **Respect Local traditions**: Respect the local culture and traditions while in Ephesus. Learn some basic Turkish words, dress modestly while visiting religious places, and be conscious of local manners.

Bruce Terry

• TRANSPORTATION OPTIONS WITHIN EPHESUS

1. **Walking:** Walking is one of the greatest methods to see Ephesus, particularly the historic city ruins. The bulk of the archaeological sites are within a very small region, making it simple to investigate on foot. Walking enables you to immerse yourself in the historical environment and see the exquisite intricacies of antique architecture up close. Remember to wear comfortable shoes, bring a drink, and protect yourself from the heat, particularly during the hot summer months.

2. **Travel Buses:** Several travel companies provide guided bus trips that explore Ephesus and adjacent sights. Tour buses are a useful choice for those who desire a planned and instructive experience. These excursions often involve experienced guides who give historical context and insights into the archaeological treasures. The trips could also include visits to other local sights like the House of the Virgin Mary or the Ephesus Archaeological Museum. However, be cautious of the time limits imposed by group trips.

3. **Taxi Services:** Taxis are widely accessible in the region of Ephesus, particularly around the main tourist sites. They provide a more flexible choice for travelers who wish to personalize their schedule and see Ephesus at their leisure. It's recommended to negotiate the fee before commencing your trip or verify that the

driver utilizes a meter. Taxis are especially handy if you have limited time or wish to visit certain sites not covered by other kinds of transportation.

4. **Dolmuş (Minibuses):** Dolmuş is a popular means of public transportation in Turkey, and it's readily accessible in Ephesus. These shared minibusses run on designated routes, linking important attractions and adjacent communities. Dolmuş is a cheap solution for budget-conscious guests and maybe a real way to see local life. Look for the signs with the destination inscribed on them or ask locals for advice on catching the appropriate Dolmuş.

5. **Rental Cars and Scooters:** For those who want more independence and flexibility in their exploration, hiring a car or scooter might be a fantastic alternative. Numerous automobile rental firms operate in the surrounding cities of Selçuk and Kusadasi, providing a selection of cars to suit various tastes and budgets. Having personal transport enables you to visit lesser-known places and explore the surrounding surroundings. However, be mindful of traffic restrictions, and local driving customs, and verify you have a valid driver's license.

6. **Horse Carriages:** For a touch of nostalgia and a unique experience, you may choose a horse-drawn carriage journey inside Ephesus. This historic type of transport adds a delightful touch to your stay, giving the impression of journeying back in time. The

carriage ride is particularly enjoyable for families and couples seeking a leisurely and romantic tour of the old city.

7. **Bicycle Rentals:** If you like riding and want a more eco-friendly method to see Ephesus, try hiring a bicycle. Many rental stores provide bicycles appropriate for varied terrains. Cycling gives a relaxing and unhurried approach to seeing the ruins and surrounding landscape. Keep in mind that parts of the terrain could be tough, so select your paths cautiously.

8. **Walking Tours:** Apart from self-directed walking, you may also join guided walking tours arranged by local companies or skilled guides. These trips appeal to varied interests, such as historical, architectural, or cultural topics. A walking tour may give in-depth information and fascinating tales about the historic city, boosting your entire experience.

Bruce Terry

CONCLUSION

In conclusion, the Ephesus Travel Guide for 2023-2024 provides a comprehensive and up-to-date resource for tourists seeking to discover one of the most historically important and awe-inspiring locations in the world. With its rich tapestry of ancient ruins, archaeological marvels, and cultural legacy, Ephesus continues to draw travelers from all parts of the world.

Throughout this book, tourists are supplied with vital information to create a memorable and pleasurable journey. From seeing the famed Library of Celsus and the majestic Grand Theater to meandering through the ancient alleyways and marveling at the Temple of Artemis, every step in Ephesus is a trip through time.

The book not only emphasizes the big locations but also goes into lesser-known jewels, enabling tourists to unearth hidden treasures and immerse themselves in the local culture. Whether it's relishing traditional Turkish food in small cafés or shopping for unique goods in busy marketplaces, Ephesus provides an intriguing combination of old-world charm and modern pleasures.

With practical recommendations on transit, lodging, and safety concerns, the book guarantees that tourists can plan their trip with confidence and simplicity. Additionally, it highlights the significance of responsible tourism, asking people to respect sensitive historical monuments and promote sustainable activities.

Bruce Terry

As the 2023-2024 Ephesus Travel Guide draws to an end, it's apparent that Ephesus stands as a tribute to human ingenuity and a living history lesson. This historic city is a must-visit location for people looking to connect with the past, immerse themselves in timeless beauty, and make memories that will last a lifetime. As tourists leave this intriguing location, they will bring with them not only memorable memories but also a better understanding of the grandeur of our common human history.